1

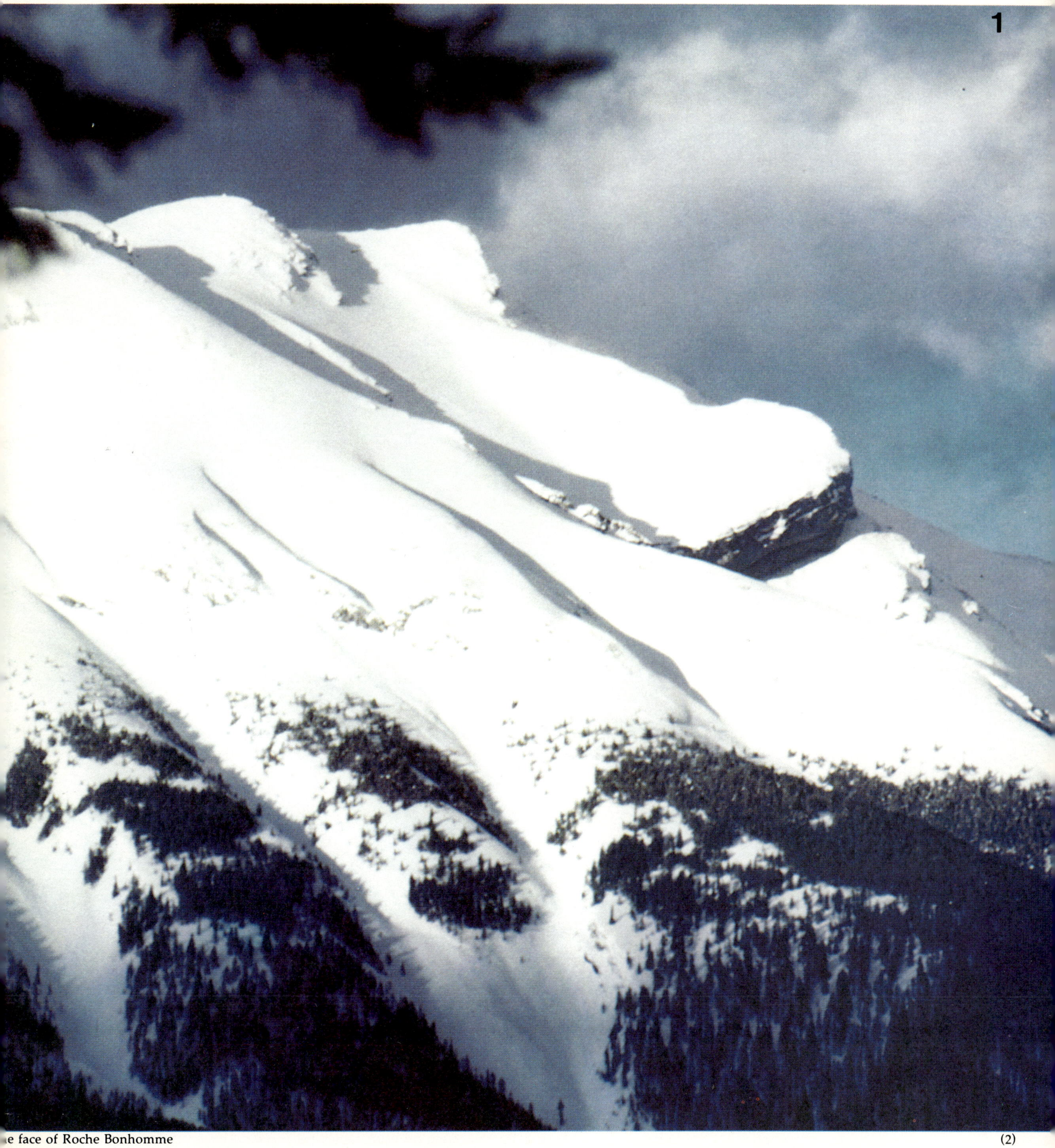

ıe face of Roche Bonhomme (2)
ıver photo: Medicine Lake in Maligne Valley (1)

The "H.M.S. Chaba" set off for a three-day exploration of the lake, Mary Schäffer perched high on a bag of flour, a slab of bacon, and a bundle of blankets. The small raft was held together with only wooden pegs and lashes, and through its yawning cracks the young woman could see fathomless icy blue waters. As the raft passed through the narrows in the lake, "There burst upon us that which all in our little company agreed was the finest view any of us had ever beheld in the Rockies." Maligne, gem of the valley, an exquisite sparkling sapphire encased in solid grey stone. It was 1908, the occasion of the first voyage on Maligne Lake.

Having arrived via Poboktan and Maligne Passes, the adventurers decided to proceed to the Athabasca Valley. Their packtrain would take the shortest route, along the Maligne River.

The outlet of the lake appeared placid. As a precaution, however, the horse selected to make the first crossing was a strong swimmer. Ricks reared in protest on being mounted. His reluctance proved to be well founded when water surged over the saddle and emptied it. Man and steed fought the angry river in vain. Caught in an undertow, Ricks was swept downstream, his rapid progress marked only by four hooves thrashing above the current. Finally, by some miracle, the dripping pair were dragged ashore. The river had deceived them.

A second attempt was made with another horse who almost drowned when his hoof caught in the halter-shank. A well named river, Maligne — wicked, cunning.

Mary Schäffer's party soon considered the name equally apt for the entire valley. Four men rode off to clear a trail. Five days later they returned to the main camp as "black as crows from burnt timber" and reported that "weeks of labour would not put us through . . . the longest way around would eventually be the shortest." They retraced their steps. An extra hundred kilometres.

Maligne, valley of the wicked river, welcomed no one. Ever reluctant to reveal the secrets of the centuries, what stories might the mountains tell of their lives?

"H.M.S. Chaba" on Maligne Lake

Pages of the Past

Some of the Maligne Valley story is written in the rocks. The layers of rock are like the pages of a book, though some may be missing or faintly written. Geologists try to interpret these stories in stone and suggest how mud changed to mountain.

Birth

Maligne began 600 million years ago, born of a shallow sea which covered this area from the Arctic to the Gulf of Mexico. Sediments were washed into this sea by rivers which flowed from the land to the east.

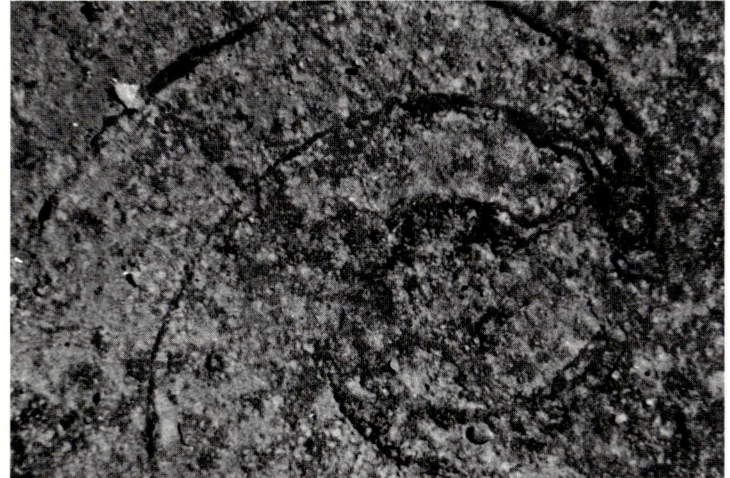

Fossilized gastropod (snail), one of many creatures that inhabited the Maligne area 350 million years ago. (4)

Layer upon layer of clays, lime muds, sand and silt sank to the bed of the ocean where the pressure of their own weight turned them to rock. Small sea creatures left impressions in the hardening wedge of sediments — fossils of snails, sea lilies and lampshells. Ripple marks from ancient waves can be seen on some rocks in the Maligne Valley, a startling testimony of their origin.

Beginning 160 million years ago, powerful forces within the crust of the earth gradually pushed this wedge of sedimentary rock layers from west to east — causing it to be compressed, folded, wrinkled and broken. Sediments made mountains.

Millions of tons of solid rock were heaved skyward, some to an angle of 60°. Sheets of rock up to 9,000 m thick were pushed six times as high as the tallest building man has ever raised.

A valley was formed where two types of mountains met, where a break or thrust fault occurred in the sheets of rock. Maligne is bounded on the northeast by the jagged ridges of the Colin and Queen Elizabeth Ranges, both included in the Front Ranges of the Rockies. The massive light-grey limestone rock contains the shells of sea animals. Some of these rock sheets dip steeply, their edges pointing skyward, like the teeth of a saw. Others are severely folded. To the southwest of Maligne Valley are the more rounded slopes of the Maligne Range, created largely of rock made from ancient shoreline sediments. These rock layers are only gently tilted, typical of mountains in the Main Ranges.

The basic plan of Maligne Valley had been drawn. It had yet to be modified.

Queen Elizabeth Range (5)

Maligne Range (6)

Youth

Lush, lazy lagoons. Steaming tropical jungles and savage swamps. Scorching sun on sturdy peaks, fresh sparkling streams. A land untried, bold and confident. Maligne and its mountains were young and wild.

As in any youth, profound and often painful changes were to be endured. Most influential in the transformation of the bedrock was water.

Each year 7500 km³ of water falls on the continents as rain and snow, creating streams and rivers of enormous energy potential.

Water has mass and can transmit energy. By simple force it can erode materials or carry them to distant shores. Water is like liquid sandpaper, transporting suspended materials which grind underlying rock, polishing it and sometimes leaving potholes.

Air bubbles in waterfalls may suddenly collapse because of changes in velocity and pressure. This violent action can cut away solid rock.

Water is a special chemical agent since it can act as a base or as an acid in chemical reactions. It is effective in chemical erosion because it can dissolve certain rocks and minerals at rapid rates. The limestone common in Maligne is water soluble and has been extensively furrowed by rain wash and snow melt. The rillenkarren produced this way in Surprise Valley are some of North America's finest examples of this feature.

Between the mountain ranges of Maligne Valley a drainage pattern began to develop. Along the thrust fault in the sheets of rock, the water eroded a channel in the youngest and softest rocks. The primitive Maligne River cut easily into the underlying limestone beds.

The mountains began to lose their youthful plumpness, as the rivers and streams quickly carried away loose rocks and small particles. When the current slackened, these materials spread out in alluvial fans in the valley.

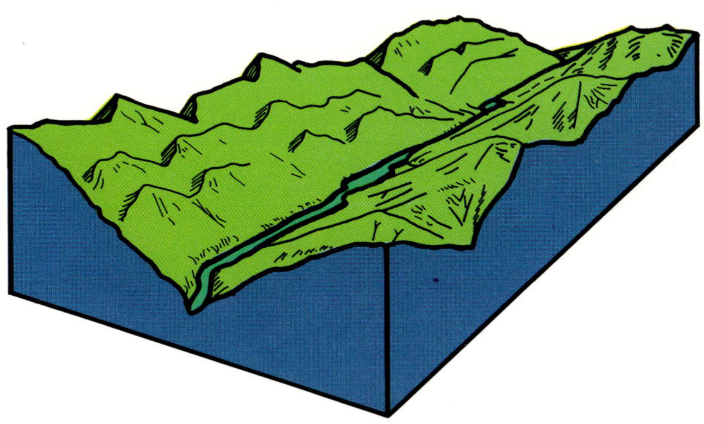

The water carved its way down into the layers of rock; the Maligne River valley became deep and narrow — a V shape.

The mountains could not stay young forever. Had they ever so deluded themselves, the mountains of Maligne were in for a COLD awakening!

Rillenkarren (7)

6 Adolescence, or the Cold Shoulder

The Ice Age began about two million years ago. More and more precipitation fell as snow, until extensive ice sheets covered more than one fifth of the earth's land surface.

Three times the ice melted and returned. The fourth and last ice advance here, the Wisconsin, ended about 10,000 years ago. Glacial ice in Maligne Valley probably came from the high mountains at its south end and flowed down to the Athabasca. Maligne Valley and its mountains were in for some relatively rapid changes. Adolescence was at hand. Time to modify appearances.

How did rivers of ice transform the features of a mountain? Glaciers carried rocks beneath them as they flowed along, filing away at the underlying bedrock. In some places the ice cut into the bedding of the rocks making them more susceptible to sliding. Glaciers scraped off much of the rock on the sides of the mountains. Once-rounded mountain structures were manicured, filed into sheer headwall cliffs and other angular shapes. Those mountains completely covered by the ice, such as the Bald Hills, were shaved of protrusions and shortened. The ice enlarged the basin where Maligne Lake now lies — 96 m deep. Glaciers widened Maligne Valley into the broad U shape that is has today.

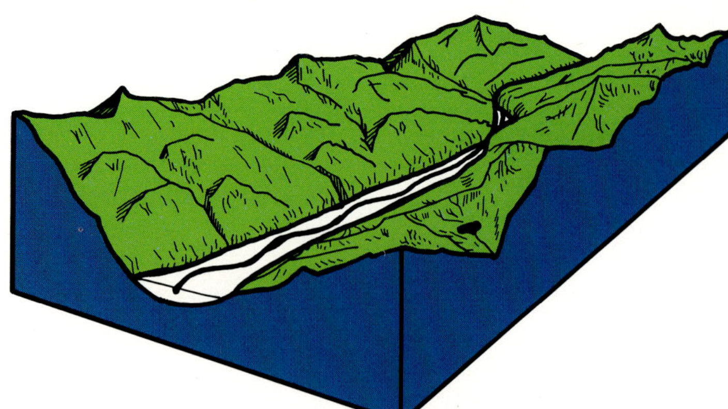

Glaciers also hauled fallen rocks on their surfaces. Most were transported out of this valley, though some were abandoned en route as the ice melted away. We call them glacial erratics. The glacial meltwaters themselves carried rock debris, which was later deposited in alluvial fans and deltas.

The last glacier to fill Maligne Valley was up to 300 m thick. As this glacier moved, it plucked up everything in its path and carried it along. Some of this mix of debris accumulated in large mounds at the front and sides of the ice to form moraines. Maligne Lake was dammed by such a moraine at its northwest end, which held back glacial meltwaters, raising the lake level.

Over the bedrock the melting glacier also scattered ground moraine — debris which had been carried on, in and beneath the glacial ice.

As the glacier receded, blocks of ice were left behind. Meltwaters buried some of them under sediments. When the blocks melted, they left depressions known as kettles. Conical mounds called kames were also formed as the glacier was melting. This accounts for the

Maligne Lake basin viewed from the south (9)

Charlton Glacier. An excellent example of a lateral moraine can be seen in the foreground. (10)

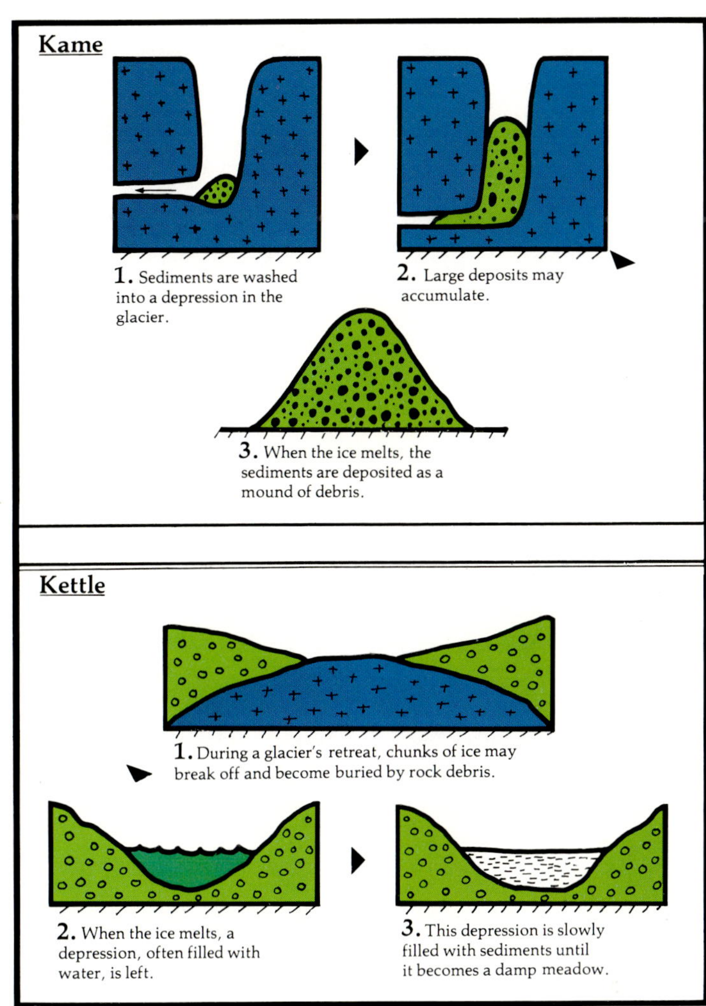

hummocks and hollows that can be seen around the north end of Maligne Lake.

Having survived a stormy adolescence, Maligne had a new image. Ten thousand years later we can still detect the lingering traces of an Ice Age, particularly in the upper reaches of the valley at the south end of Maligne Lake.

(11) The valley is still adjusting to some of the extreme landscapes created. Many large rocks can be found on the valley floor today, evidence of slides that occur in reaction to instabilities left by the glaciers.

Maligne is now thought to be in a post-glacial era. But as in centuries past, North American climates once again have become moister and cooler. Could another ice age be coming? The mountains of Maligne remain mute on the subject.

Maturity — the marks of distinction

The mountains continued to change, to mature. Adolescence had been a comparatively short stage in their lives. It was now time to mold some of the special features that had been initiated, those which would make Maligne Valley unique. In this undertaking, water was reinstated as the primary agent of erosion.

Maligne Canyon   (12)   (13 above)   (14)

A bit of sculpture

One of the major sculpturing processes in the valley has taken about 10,000 years and, in fact, continues at present. You can see the forces of nature labouring on site, any day of the year. Their progress is slow; they cut down into the rock at a rate of only half a centimetre per year. But they persist, never missing a day of work in centuries.

Many factors contributed to the carving of this gorge. Glacial ice had gouged out a deeper basin in the Athabasca Valley leaving the lip of Maligne Valley hanging about 120 m above the floor of the Athabasca. Therefore, the waters of the Maligne Valley followed a steep gradient as they flowed down into the Athabasca. Falling water has a forceful impact and cutting was encouraged by the generosity of the melting glaciers. The sculpture began.

The Maligne River surges through this spectacular gorge before joining the Athabasca River on its journey to the Arctic Ocean. The canyon is a new river channel, eroded since the ice sheets retreated from this region. A moraine deposited by glacial ice diverted the Maligne River northwards to the present location of the canyon, forcing it to flow over limestone rock. Water flow was restricted to a narrow area. The pattern of small cracks in the rock, which developed along zones of weakness, controlled the water's path. The river was forced to make some sharp 60 to 90 degree bends, which are apparent in the present canyon.

The cold grey cliffs of the canyon — up to 30 times the height of a man — seem to testify to the strength and stability of the rock. Yet, at the hand of water, the rock dissolved and cracks in the earth yawned.

Mechanical abrasion by water has also worn away some of the bedrock. In the many potholes, or circular depressions, suspended sediments have been captured. The rapid current will keep them circling, grinding the limestone, until the river sinks farther down and abandons the potholes forever.

Frost plays a minor role in the continuing erosion of the canyon. Water vapour in cracks condenses to form a feathery deposit of ice. In this process the water expands and may cause small pieces of rock to flake off the walls.

There is much to discover in the canyon. It is one of three places in Alberta where black swifts are known to nest. Mosses and ferns live in potholes in the rock. Fossils from the ancient sea world are common.

In the lower section of Maligne Canyon it seems that the river flow greatly exceeds that in the upper gorge, less than a thousand metres upstream. But is that possible?

Almost anything is possible in Maligne Valley . . .

(15)
Maligne Canyon in winter

(16)
Exploring one of the other canyons in the Maligne Valley (17)

The leaky bathtub

Summer visitors assume that Medicine is a normal mountain lake. But local Indians spoke of it as Bad Medicine. Its strange disappearance spelled foreboding. Again the mountains whisper of the wickedness of Maligne.

For part of each year the lake disappears, becoming a clay flat with only scattered pools of water connected by a stream. The Maligne River continues to enter its southeast end, but no surface outlet from the basin is visible at the other end. The water vanishes into the lake bottom.

Medicine Lake is like a bathtub without a plug. The Maligne River pours into it from the south, where it drains down into rubble and boulders at various locations along the north shore. The water streams through underground plumbing — thought to be a maze of caves and passages formed in the easily dissolvable limestone rock. Most of the sinking river rises to the surface again in the area of Maligne Canyon, 16 km down the valley. The flow time to these outlets is a minimum of 16 hours.

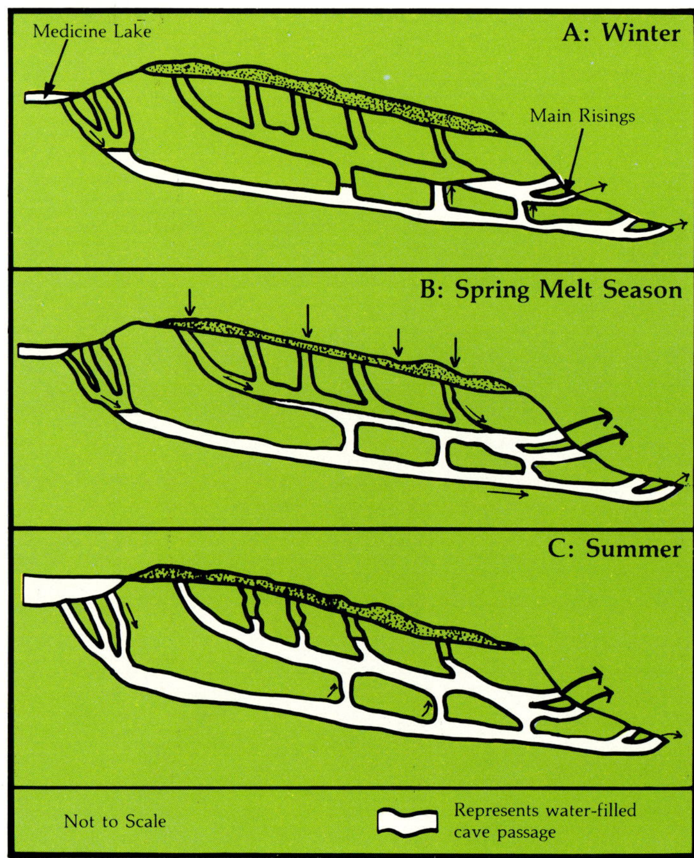

The largest springs are in Maligne Canyon, where they issue from small caves which are flooded in summer and largely blocked with rubble in winter. So there is truth to the notion that more water flows in the lower canyon than the upper.

Medicine Lake in summer
(18)

In fall and winter Medicine Lake is nearly empty — most of the water has flowed out of the bathtub. With summer melting of glacier ice and snow, the Maligne River swells. As the water rushes into Medicine Lake, the sink points reach their capacity and the lake level rises; the flow from the tap has exceeded the capacity of the drain.

The tub begins to fill and Medicine Lake spreads. It may rise until it overflows into a normally dry surface channel at its north end.

It is thought that this remarkable system was created before the last glaciation but was modified by it. For example, glacial deposits probably clogged the underground plumbing and developed the surface drainage path for runoff. But this is not the only uncertainty which scientists have recently been investigating at Medicine Lake.

It was a French scientist, Professor Jean Corbel, who first recognized the existence of the sinking river when he visited the area in 1956. Ten years later a group from McMaster University began studies in Maligne Basin. Using special dyes, they accomplished the first successful tracing of water from Medicine Lake to the outlets, visible proof of underground passages. But an entrance to the system hasn't been located. Scientists have taken resistivity measurements and have used infrared imagery; they've even drilled for the tunnels. But access to the system has eluded all investigators.

The Maligne River is one of the largest known sinking rivers in the Western Hemisphere. One researcher suggests that the Maligne system may contain one of the largest inaccessible cave systems anywhere in the world.

Local residents have long suspected underground passages at Medicine Lake. Park Warden Micky McGuire was fascinated by it. In the 1930s he tried to "either see where the water went or block the sinks". He dumped two truckloads of *Saturday Evening Post* magazines into the sinks and, later, a truckload of mattresses. Park officials even considered building a dam on the lake to prevent its disappearance and thus improve fishing. They rejected the idea when they realized how much fill would be required.

Maligne was triumphant. Mere mortals would not alter nature's plans for the valley. If she decided to conceal the entrances to the amazing underground network, so be it.

The sinking river will continue to enlarge its underground passages, so that one day it may be able to handle the entire flow from Maligne River. And Medicine Lake may then disappear forever . . .

Medicine Lake at low water (19)

A large spring in Maligne Canyon (20 above)

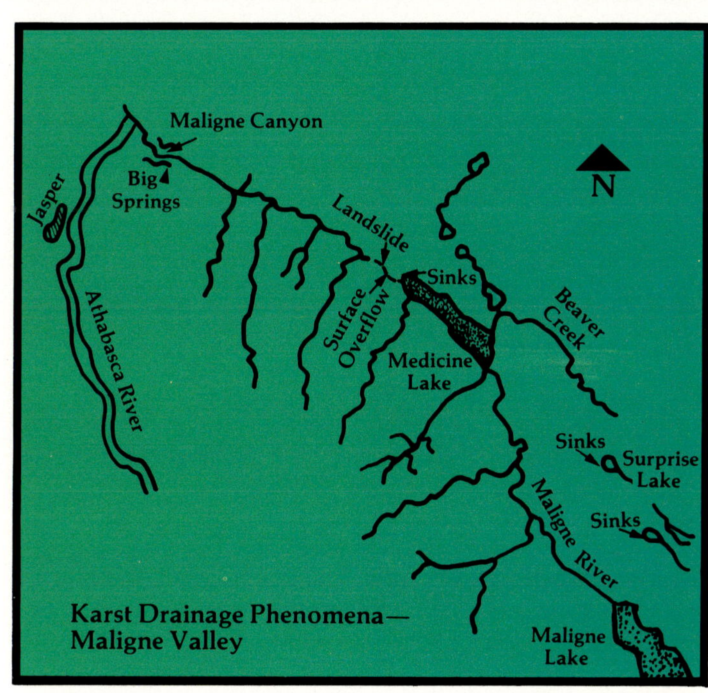

Drainage in the nearby Surprise Valley has been found to be completely underground via two small sinking lakes and various other smaller sinks. These may drain into Medicine Lake.

The sink points at the north end of Medicine Lake are visible by the end of October. (21)

erflow channel north of Medicine Lake (22)

Fluorescent dye being released into Medicine Lake (23)

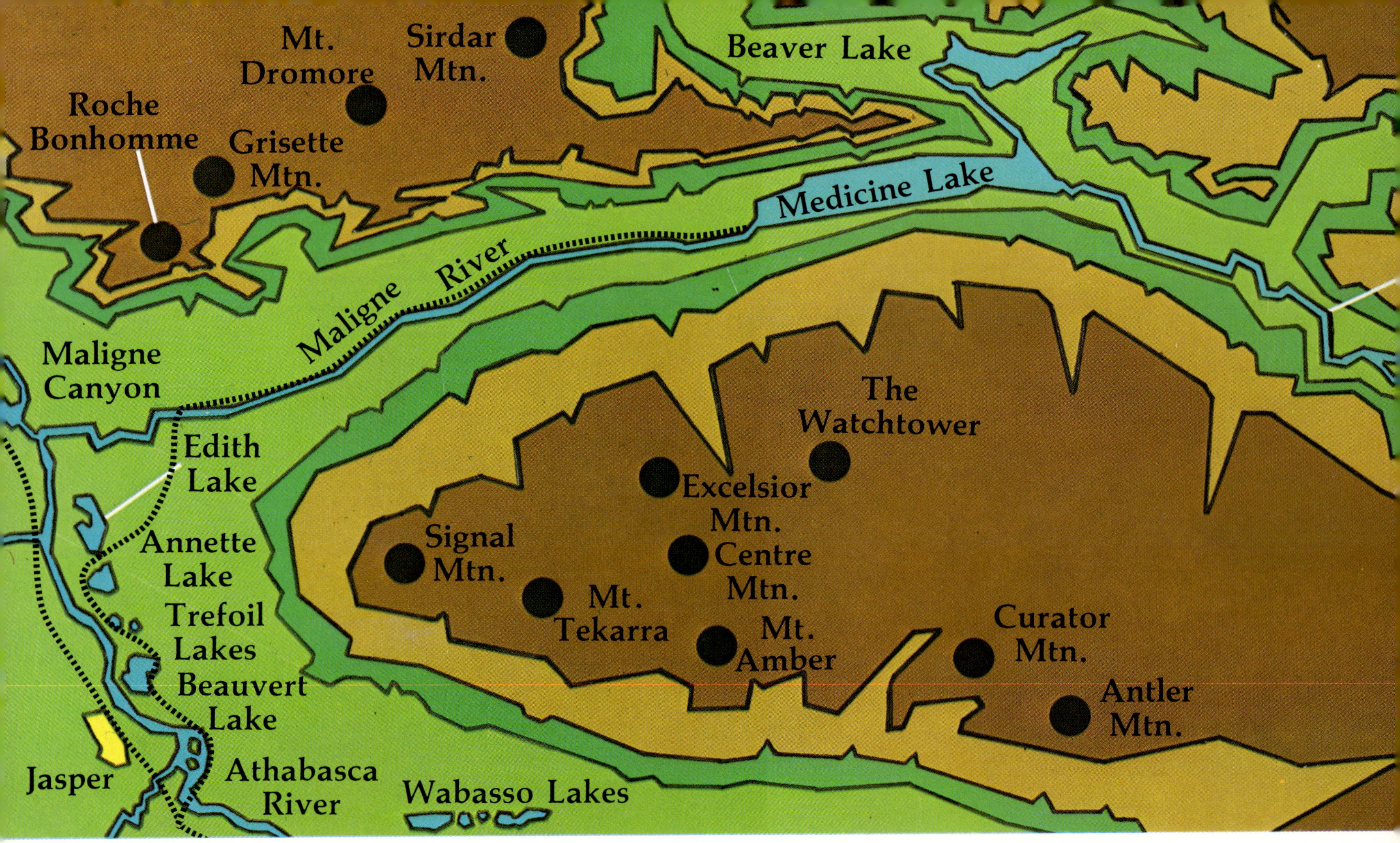

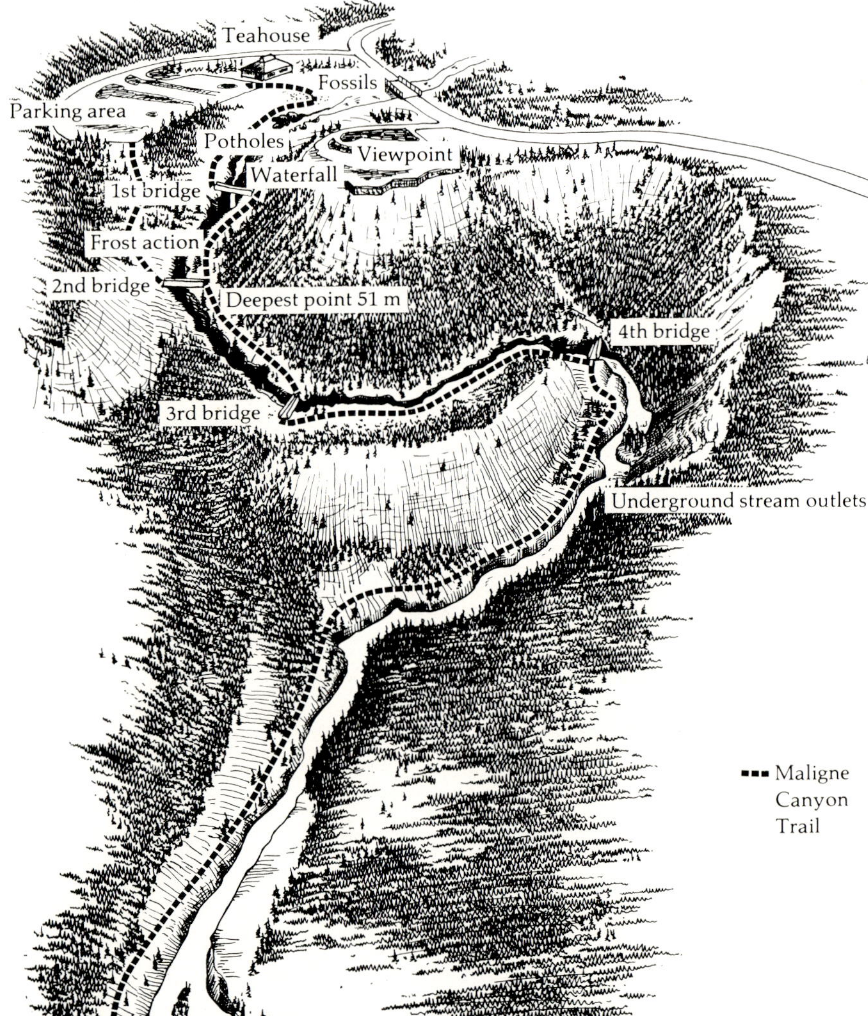

Exploring Maligne Valley

Maligne Canyon

—Examine the exhibit which explains how the Maligne Valley has developed and the changes which are taking place today.

—Follow the trail along the canyon and learn how it was formed.

Along the Maligne Road

—Stop at pulloffs along the way. Signs identify landscape features and explain their origin.

—Tune your radio dial to 1490 (English) or 1230 (French) for up-to-date information on what to see and do in the valley.

Medicine Lake

—The exhibit at the north end of the lake explains how the water level is affected by the presence of the Maligne Valley's great underground river.

Maligne Lake

—Walk to Schäffer viewpoint for a good view down the lake and a chance to learn about the early travellers to the area.

—Walk the short trail to the Hummock and Hollow Meadow and examine excellent examples of kames and kettles.

—Visit the lakeside exhibit, for a better understanding of Maligne Lake.

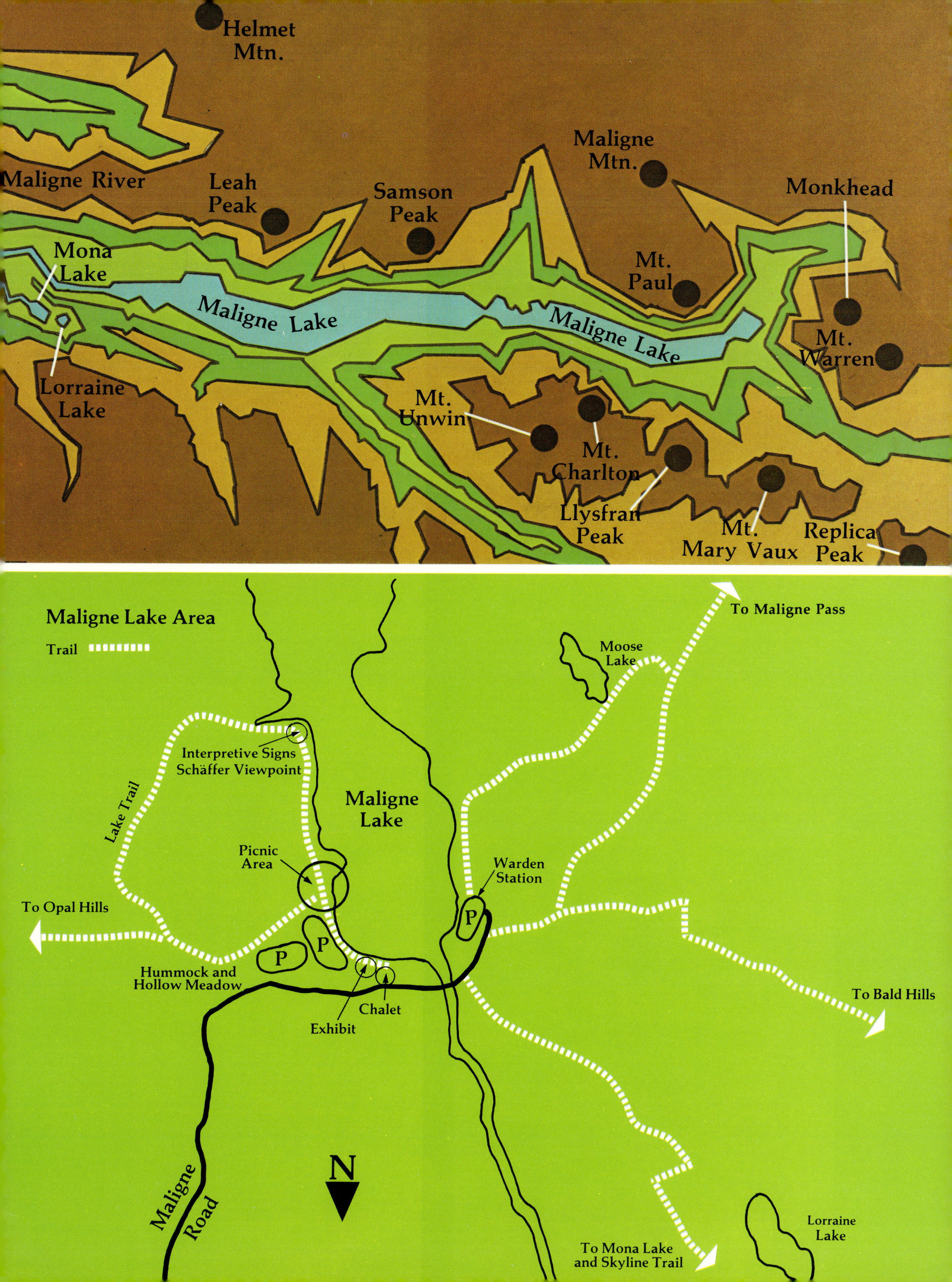
Helmet Mtn.
Maligne River
Leah Peak
Samson Peak
Maligne Mtn.
Monkhead
Mona Lake
Maligne Lake
Maligne Lake
Mt. Paul
Mt. Warren
Lorraine Lake
Mt. Unwin
Mt. Charlton
Llysfran Peak
Mt. Mary Vaux
Replica Peak
Maligne Lake Area
Trail
To Maligne Pass
Moose Lake
Interpretive Signs
Schäffer Viewpoint
Lake Trail
Maligne Lake
Picnic Area
Warden Station
P
To Opal Hills
P
P
Hummock and Hollow Meadow
Chalet
Exhibit
To Bald Hills
Maligne Road
N
To Mona Lake and Skyline Trail
Lorraine Lake

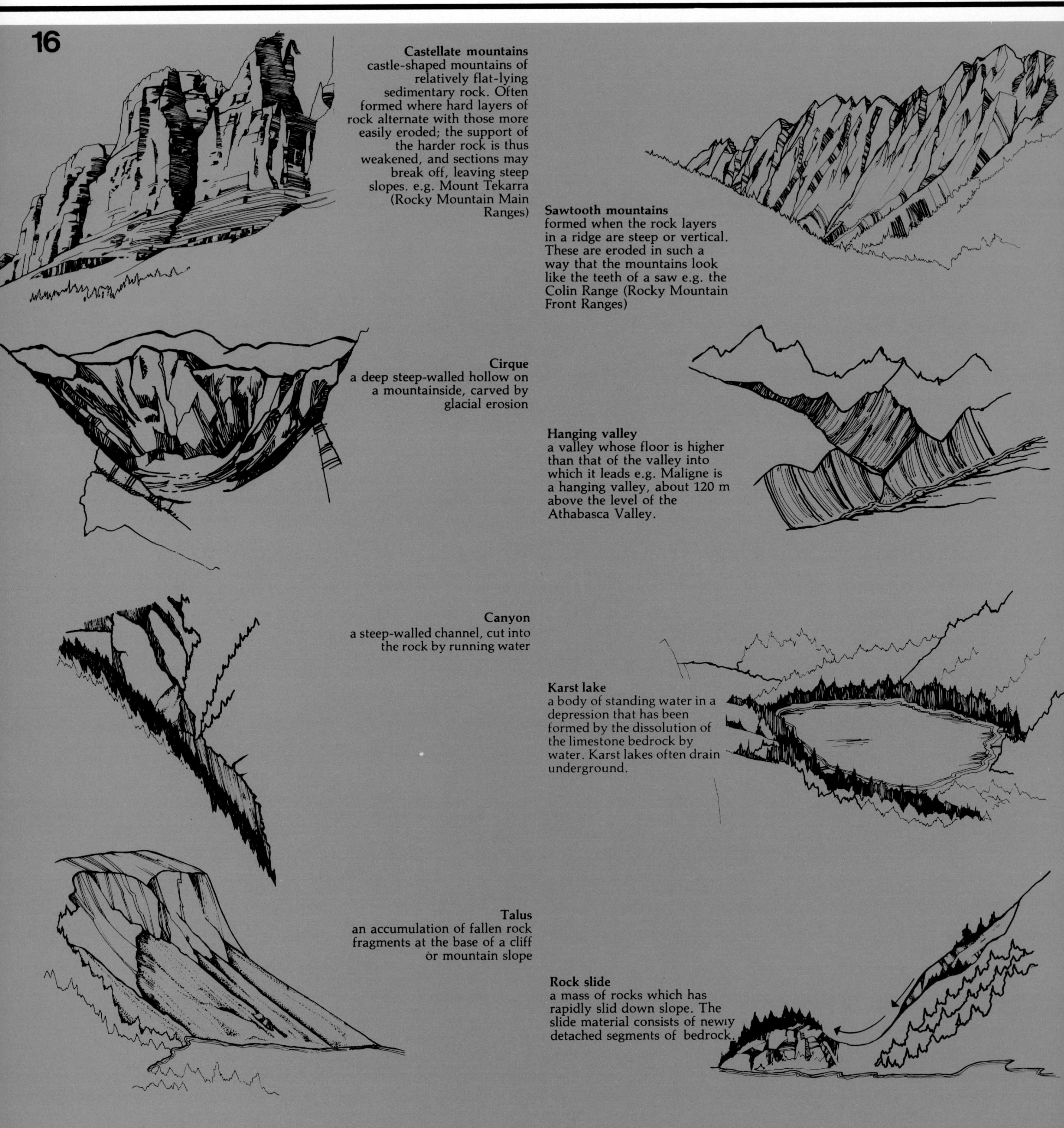

Castellate mountains
castle-shaped mountains of relatively flat-lying sedimentary rock. Often formed where hard layers of rock alternate with those more easily eroded; the support of the harder rock is thus weakened, and sections may break off, leaving steep slopes. e.g. Mount Tekarra (Rocky Mountain Main Ranges)

Sawtooth mountains
formed when the rock layers in a ridge are steep or vertical. These are eroded in such a way that the mountains look like the teeth of a saw e.g. the Colin Range (Rocky Mountain Front Ranges)

Cirque
a deep steep-walled hollow on a mountainside, carved by glacial erosion

Hanging valley
a valley whose floor is higher than that of the valley into which it leads e.g. Maligne is a hanging valley, about 120 m above the level of the Athabasca Valley.

Canyon
a steep-walled channel, cut into the rock by running water

Karst lake
a body of standing water in a depression that has been formed by the dissolution of the limestone bedrock by water. Karst lakes often drain underground.

Talus
an accumulation of fallen rock fragments at the base of a cliff or mountain slope

Rock slide
a mass of rocks which has rapidly slid down slope. The slide material consists of newly detached segments of bedrock.

Alluvial fan
a cone-shaped deposit of debris carried by a stream down a steep channel. As it reaches level ground, the stream spreads out and slows, dropping suspended material. A **delta** is a similar formation deposited underwater.

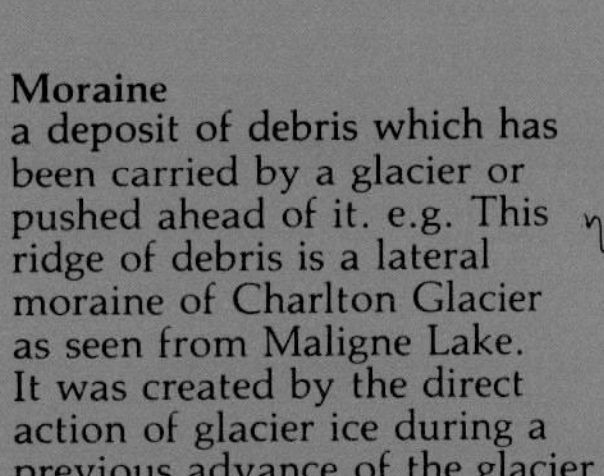

Moraine
a deposit of debris which has been carried by a glacier or pushed ahead of it. e.g. This ridge of debris is a lateral moraine of Charlton Glacier as seen from Maligne Lake. It was created by the direct action of glacier ice during a previous advance of the glacier.

Avalanche slope
an incline where a mass of snow, sometimes containing rock, soil and ice, has moved rapidly down slope. Avalanche slopes are usually treeless, and bear low resilient vegetation that can survive the force of a snow avalanche. Most of the slope cover is pushed into a pile of rocks, branches and mud.

Erratic
a rock fragment, usually of boulder size, which has been carried by glacial ice and deposited at some distance from its origin

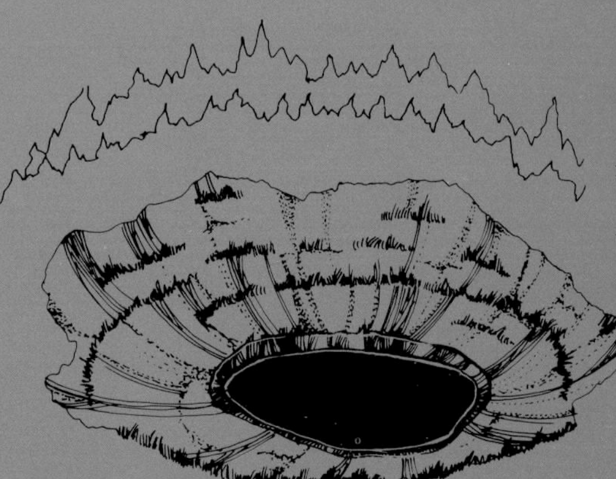

Kettle
a bowl-shaped depression formed where a large block of ice broke off from the front of a receding glacier. Glacial sediments surrounded the block, which melted and left a kettle-shaped hole in the ground.

Rock glacier
A glacier-like tongue of angular rock debris cemented together by ice. When fragments from the cliffs above are added to it, the increased weight forces the rock glacier to creep sluggishly down slope.

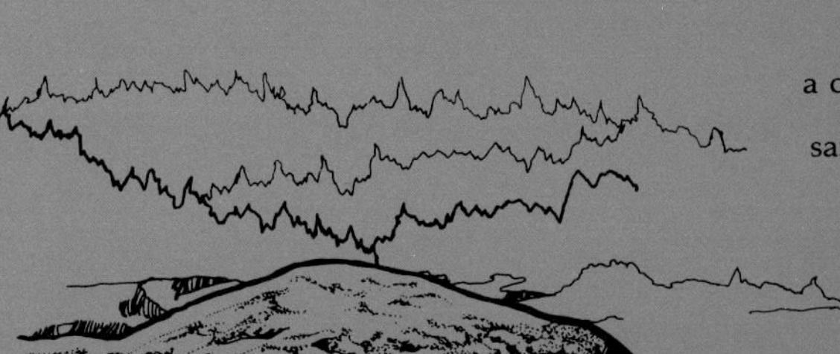

Kame
a conical hill or short irregular ridge of glacial gravel and sand, deposited by meltwaters in or on melting glacial ice. When the ice melted, sediments were left behind, forming mounds.

Aging

Each day the mountains greet the dawn with a new face. The aging process never ceases.

Maligne River flows fast and furiously. Even the rubbish heaps of the glaciers and discarded fragments from the mountain slopes have not stopped it. Faster, faster, faster, cutting and eroding, pausing as it approaches its vanishing point at Medicine Lake.

Countless other streams pour down the slopes of the Maligne mountains to the valley bottom. They too leave their marks — canyons in the mountainsides.

The rivers and streams of Maligne often carry a heavy load of sediments, especially in spring meltwaters. As the current slows, these materials are usually dropped to form alluvial fans and deltas. There are two of these deposits at Samson Narrows in Maligne Lake, and they are gradually filling in the basin, narrowing the gap. It may one day be closed, and the lake cut in two.

In the same way that frost erodes the Maligne Canyon, the freezing and thawing of water in cracks breaks off rock fragments on the mountainsides of Maligne Valley.

Loose red rock fragments tumble down the slopes, and large unstable sheets of stone often result in slides. Two major rock slides exist in Maligne Valley. These are located along Maligne Lake 3 km from the northwest end and at the northwest end of Medicine Lake. The slide debris forms a pile 250 m high.

Winter is not a time of inactivity. Avalanches of ice and snow sweep down the gullies, ripping up full-grown trees in their path.

The thunder of avalanches can be heard any time of the year at the south end of Maligne Lake. The mountains here still cradle a complex of glaciers and icefields; a mere souvenir from the Ice Age, their meltwaters produce a significant feature — Maligne Lake. Maligne is the largest glacier-fed lake in the Canadian Rockies — 27.5 km long. With glaciers supplying its water, Maligne Lake doesn't invite swimmers.

The Maligne glaciers also take partial credit for the color of the water. Suspended glacial silt reflects blue and green light from the spectrum thus giving the water its aquamarine tint.

Although the ice sheets have long disappeared, the Maligne glaciers actively influence the valley today.

Water, frost, ice and snow — all working together — sculpting the landscape of Maligne Valley and its mountains. No wonder the mountains are showing their age! The processes that occur here are but a sampling of those which are continuing to modify the entire Rocky Mountain landscape.

Maligne River (24)

This natural arch, a few kilometres south of Medicine Lake was formed by frost action. (25)

Harebell (26)

A Land for the Living

The oldest rocks in Maligne Valley contain traces of marine life which lived 600 million years ago, long before the valley was formed. Today's living communities of Maligne are relatively recent arrivals. They began moving in about 10,000 years ago when the valley glaciers melted away.

Today, a few grassy meadows and lodgepole pine cover the lower regions of the valley. Around Maligne Canyon there are even some Douglas fir where warmth and dryness permit their growth.

Most of the lower valley is now covered by a forest of lodgepole pine, the result of fire in the 1890s. Its burning breath burst open the cones of existing pines, and their seeds sprouted in the charred earth. In the shade of the pine grow the Engelmann spruce, which are gradually taking over. Within this forested subalpine area there are also avalanche slopes, wetlands and river bottoms which host a diversity of plant and animal life.

At about 2130 m the forest thins out, and the force of wind and weather stunts and bends existing clumps of trees. Higher up the slopes is a touch of the Arctic misplaced — the alpine tundra, where trees are absent. Here the soil is shallow, often unstable. Vegetation must challenge high winds and cold temperatures, avalanches and alternating flood and drought. In the alpine there is a world of plants, each specially equipped to do battle with Maligne, the unmerciful valley.

Plant communities in turn influence which animal populations can survive in a particular region of Maligne. Caribou are among the residents of the alpine tundra. These mountain caribou thrive in Maligne, having adapted to its harshness. By November they seek the shelter of mature forests and may venture onto

Coyote tracks in the mud in the Medicine Lake basin (27)

Douglas fir forest (28)

The alpine meadows of the Opal Hills (29)

alluvial fans and deltas, such as at Medicine Lake, in search of readily available vegetation. In spring they move back to the alpine tundra and a diet of lichens — just one example of a life regulated by the seasons of Maligne. The herds here roam some of the most southerly caribou range in the Canadian Rockies. An indicator of true wilderness, caribou do not linger in an area frequented by people.

Timber wolves, fishers and wolverines also populate tracts of land where humans seldom venture. Maligne Valley supports only a small population of grizzly bears, although a Maligne warden once came across three different sows with their cubs during a one-hour horseback ride.

Moose are a common sight as they feed on the river bottoms and wetlands. Often they browse on shrubs and small trees in open meadows near Maligne Lake. You may even glimpse a family outing — a mother with twins in tow.

Mule deer too are quite numerous, and elk graze in the lower valley.

Maligne also has 67 kinds of resident or breeding birds, and about 50 more migrants and incidentals. Most live in the forest-tundra zones; trees and shrubs serve as sites for nests and escape, while the tundra provides food. Hummingbirds, warblers, great gray owls and goshawks may be seen. Ducks nest on Maligne Lake, when it is finally ice free at the beginning of June. Some of the young may still be flightless in early October but must take to their wings by freeze-up in mid-November. Maligne has no compassion, she makes no exceptions for laggards.

Although Maligne Lake is the largest body of water in Jasper National Park, it has no native populations of fish. Another bit of trickery: the Maligne Canyon and underground sections of Maligne River are natural barriers to colonizing fish. But those fishermen on Maligne Lake are not waiting for eternity. Stocking began in 1928, with brook trout and later rainbow. The stocking procedure has now been discontinued in favor of maintaining naturally reproducing populations of fish.

In Maligne Valley there are even unusual insects that can cope with its severe conditions. The Grylloblatta is a rare insect that is restricted to high altitudes because it can only survive in a very narrow temperature range near freezing.

Maligne, a multitude of plant and animal communities, each suited to an environment created by these mountains and their valley.

It is a life of struggle. But the design of nature was a complex one and governed valley residents with impartiality. The arrival of man, however, raised the possibility of a threat to it all.

Rock barrens on the summit of Signal Mountain (30)

Calypso orchid (31)

ireweed (33) Moose feeding in Maligne Lake (34) Indian paintbrush (35)

Horses packing bedsprings
into the chalet at
Maligne Lake,
1936

The Challengers

The faces of stone continued their watch. For close to 100 million years they had been the silent sentinels of the valley. The mountains did not welcome the first intruders.

The human history of the valley is a chronicle of challenges to the conspiracy of Maligne, valley of wickedness and trickery.

The plot was long successful. Natives rarely ventured into the Maligne. The only record of their passing was the isolated find of a stone axe and the legend of Bad Medicine.

It was not until 1811 that Athabasca Pass, newly discovered gateway to the Pacific, lured fur traders to the Jasper area. Riding horseback along the east banks of the Athabasca River, the fur brigades were forced to cross the mouth of the Maligne River. Upended packhorses and soggy provisions testified to the current's authority and initiated the reputation of "la rivière maligne" — the wicked river. It was actually a Jesuit priest from Belgium, Father de Smet, who first recorded the name; he visited the region in 1846.

No white man headed up the Maligne Valley until John A. MacDonald conceived his national dream — a continental railroad for the new nation of Canada. In 1875 the Canadian Pacific Railway sent a surveyor to determine the feasibility of a route through the Maligne Valley. Henry MacLeod's impressions of the trip to the head of the valley were such that, apparently unmoved by the charms of Maligne Lake, he referred to it as Sorefoot Lake! There would be no train whistles heard here. The area waited more than a quarter of a century to be further explored — by a Quaker in buckskin.

The Stoney Indians knew her as Yahe-Weha, the mountain woman. She was introduced to the Canadian Rockies as a girl of 19, aboard the railroad that Henry MacLeod helped to survey. Mary Schäffer was a wealthy Quaker from Pennsylvania and the wife of a prominent Philadelphia botanist.

Widowed in her early thirties, she continued to spend summers in the Banff area, yet longed to ride northward on the heels of the explorers. Despite the protests of disbelieving family and friends, she and her friend, Mary Adams, hired themselves a guide. Billy Warren would teach them the tricks of the trail, beginning with horseback riding. One of their expeditions would be a search for Chaba Imne, a mysterious lake in the heart of the Rockies . . .

The legendary lake was described to Mary Schäffer by Stoney Indian Samson Beaver, who drew her a rough map on a grubby bit of paper. In 1908 her packtrain headed north from Laggan (Lake Louise): 22 horses, six riders and Muggins the dog. Mary Schäffer became the first white woman to see Maligne Lake, when her group reached it from the south end.

The old Indian trails soon beckoned her back. In 1911, Mary Schäffer returned to complete a survey of the lake. Authorities in the newly established Jasper National Park agreed to ease her trip by blazing a trail from Fitzhugh (Jasper).

The Otto brothers accepted the challenge, even agreeing to transport five-metre timbers for Mary's boat. They guided her up Wabasso Creek, to a snow-locked pass. Spruce trees became necessary shovels. These were left jammed in the snow to mark the new route — Shovel Pass. Another conquest.

In the same year A.O. Wheeler, government topographer and president of the Alpine Club of Canada, led an expedition up the Maligne Valley. Even the Smithsonian Institute sent representatives. The physical characteristics of Maligne would be duly noted. Photographer Byron Harmon accompanied the group, as did world-famous alpinist Conrad Kain from Austria. The mountain peaks themselves would be challenged.

The Maligne conspiracy proved ineffective against the increasing onslaught. A rough trail had been hewn up the valley to Maligne Lake, to which visitors rode in the packtrains of local outfitters Fred Brewster and Curly Phillips. Among those who packed and wrangled horses were Mona Matheson and sister Agnes — the first female guides in Jasper National Park.

Fred Brewster beside the boat packed into Maligne Lake for Mary Schäffer by the Otto brothers   (37)

Soon, the first sector of the route could be travelled by vehicle: cars to Medicine Lake, and across it by boat. When completed by packtrain this was advertised as "less than a ten-hour trip". Eventually horsedrawn buckboards and Brewster's old model Buicks could take visitors right up to Maligne Lake, where a rustic lodge awaited them.

There was another chalet at Medicine Lake, and a tea room had been operating at Maligne Canyon since the early 1920s. Boating and fishing services were available at Medicine, Beaver, Mona and Maligne Lakes. Skiing with a guide on nearby glaciers was another attraction.

Maligne lured adventurers from every corner of the globe. A 1926 pow-wow of trail riders included a renowned Japanese alpinist. The Alpine Club pitched camp at Maligne Lake on its 1930 expedition — with more than 150 members representing many countries. Seven first ascents were made, many under the direction of professional Swiss guides Hans and Henry Fuhrer.

Relief labour projects in the Dirty Thirties gifted the reluctant valley with a gravel road from Maligne Canyon to Medicine Lake. But a return trip from Maligne Lake by horseback, via Shovel Pass and Wabasso, was still popular. Fred Brewster cruised the ranges for years in search of a more spectacular way to drop back into the Athabasca Valley. On the tops of the mountains he found his trail. It awaited its first riders in 1937, and today backpackers discover the thrills of the Skyline Trail. The narrow path winds across the alpine tundra, as high as 2530 m. From the trail, hikers can see an endless sea of jagged snowy peaks visible to the west, including the highest in the Canadian Rockies, Mount Robson.

In 1969, a modern road was constructed for the entire route up the valley to Maligne Lake, now accessible to the world. Visitors may not find the "untouched land" that Mary Schäffer described, nor the "great unlonely silence of the wilderness", yet Maligne remains relatively unspoiled.

Mary Schäffer
(38)

Mountain Memoirs

If the lifetime of these mountains could be compressed into a year, then the relative time of man in the valley would be only a matter of seconds.

Men now walk in the shadows of the mountains and carry with them the power to choose between preserving and destroying wonders that nature has taken millions of years to create. Maligne Valley is one of the special places that exist in the world today. Because Maligne is part of a national park, there is hope that this irreplaceable heritage will not be spent.

But the battle for preservation is not easily won. When A.O. Wheeler visited Maligne Lake in 1911, he noted the abundance of wildlife, especially bighorn sheep and goats. Yet he issued a warning, "It will readily be seen that to preserve these wild animals in their native habitat will prove of infinitely greater value to the country than to advertise them as spoils of the chase, when they will soon cease to exist." Hunting, mining and logging were still permitted in the new Jasper National Park.

Regulations evolved to maintain the entire park in as natural a state as possible, but even these may be insufficient. The caribou population in Maligne Valley is diminishing, as man penetrates deeper into their domain. The solutions to such problems as this are not always evident, for to us the fragility and complexity of nature are difficult to comprehend . . . perhaps a clue to the Maligne conspiracy. Was it born of the fear that men would become the trustees of such a valuable heritage as Maligne? Perhaps this too the mountains knew.

The mountains of Maligne have seen much. They are named in honour of events witnessed in their lifetime. Maligne Mountain itself whispers of French voyageurs who were reluctant to tackle a wicked river, and Mt. Henry MacLeod remembers a disappointed surveyor. Samson and Leah are tributes to the Indian and his squaw who provided directions to Chaba Imne. A notable peak is Mt. Unwin, scaled by a packer on Mary Schäffer's expedition; from this mountain he first

Colin Range

Tour boats take visitors to the south end of Maligne Lake. (40)

sighted Maligne Lake. Mt. Warren was named in recognition of the grit and determination of her chief guide whom she later married. Mary Schäffer herself named most of these mountains.

"I suppose I am too little a boy to have a mountain of my own," remarked nine-year-old nephew Paul. He accompanied Mary when she returned to Maligne Lake in 1911. During his visit, he was the first to climb an un-named peak on the east side of the lake. Aunt Mary recorded it as Mt. Paul.

Names — a legacy of adventurers who once followed old Indian trails in this valley of the wicked river. The mountain memoirs have a new chapter.

Yet the faces of stone are still silent. Geologists have attempted to piece together the story of Maligne, but the mysteries remain.

Spirit Island (41)

Camping on the Skyline Trail

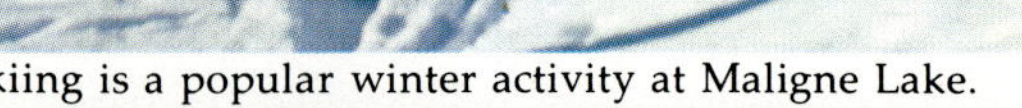

Skiing is a popular winter activity at Maligne Lake.

aligne, valley of the wicked river

32 Published by authority of the Honourable John Fraser,
Minister of the Environment
En Publication No. QS-W118-000-EE-A1
© Minister of Supply and Services Canada, 1979
Cat. No. R62-111/1979
ISBN 0-660-10468-7
Price $2.00

Credits
Author Merna M. Forster for Parks Canada
Photographs courtesy of Archives of the Canadian Rockies (3, 38)
        Jasper Yellowhead Historical Society (36, 37)
    and for Parks Canada,
        Rene Belland (1)
        Karen Friskney (8)
        Dave Huddlestone (17, 18)
        Marg Letts (35)
        Len Magee (9, 11, 12, 40)
        Dave Pick (28)
        John Pitcher (16, 41)
        Keith Richards (2, 31, 32)
        Jim Todgham (4, 5, 6, 7, 10, 13, 14, 15, 19, 20, 21,
            22, 23, 24, 25, 26, 27, 29, 30, 33, 34, 39, 42, 43, 44)
Design and Illustration by
Hill, Miller & Hutchins, Communications Consultants Ltd., Calgary, Alberta

Further Explorations

You may see other examples of geological features and processes described in this publication at the places listed below.

1. **Maligne Valley:**
   Surprise Valley — sink lakes, rock slide and
     rillenkarren
   Bald Hills — view of Maligne Lake and surrounding
     peaks
   Opal Hills — view of Surprise Valley
   Opal Peak — effects of frost wedging
   Skyline Trail — cirques, avalanche slopes,
     moraines, frost hummocks, glacial erratics
   Mona Lake — kettles and kames
2. **Other places in Jasper National Park:**
   **Athabasca, Sunwapta, Punchbowl and Tangle
     Falls** — waterfalls
   Columbia Icefield — glaciers and icefields,
     moraines
   Jonas Creek — rock slide along Icefields Parkway
   Terminal Mountain — rock glacier
   Fiddle and Sunwapta Rivers — canyons
3. **Other Parks:**
   Waterton — Red Rock Canyon
   Yoho — Upper Yoho Valley, for variety of features
   Banff — Johnston Canyon, Victoria Glacier

Further Readings

Baird, David M. *Jasper National Park, Behind the
  Mountains and Glaciers.* Edmonton: Hurtig, 1977.
Hardy, W.G. (ed.) *Alberta. A Natural History.*
  Edmonton: Hurtig, 1967.
Shelton, John S. *Geology Illustrated.* San Francisco:
  Freeman, 1966.